Mrs. Christine Kosinski

BUBBLE GUM

written by
H. I. Peeples

illustrated by
Thomas Payne

A Calico Book
Published by Contemporary Books, Inc.
CHICAGO · NEW YORK

Library of Congress Cataloging-in-Publication Data
Peeples, H. I.
Bubble gum / H. I. Peeples : illustrated by Tom Payne.
p.   cm. — (Where does this come from?)
"A Calico book."
Summary: Traces the origins of bubble gum, describing its
discovery, processing, composition, and international appeal.
ISBN 0-8092-4409-8 : $6.95
1. Bubble gum—Juvenile literature.   [1. Bubble gum.   2. Chewing gum.]
I. Payne, Tom, ill.   II. Title.
III. Series: Peeples, H. I.   Where does this come from?
TX799.P44   1989
641.3′3—dc19   88-29190
                                                                          CIP
                                                                           AC

Published by Contemporary Books, Inc.
180 North Michigan Avenue, Chicago, Illinois 60601
Manufactured in the United States of America
Library of Congress Catalog Card Number: 88-29190
International Standard Book Number: 0-8092-4409-8

Published simultaneously in Canada by Beaverbooks, Ltd.
195 Allstate Parkway, Valleywood Business Park
Markham, Ontario L3R 4T8 Canada

It's a marble . . . it's a balloon . . . it's a BUBBLE! The biggest bubble-gum bubble ever blown was twenty-two inches around! You've probably blown some good-sized ones yourself, but could you blow one that large? And have you ever wondered where those chewy blobs known as bubble gum come from?

Before there was bubble gum, there was chewing gum. And the story of chewing gum begins thousands of years ago, when cavepeople chewed wads of tree sap.

Since then, practically everyone has found something to chew, including the ancient Greeks, the Mayan Indians, and many others. Indians in New England gave the first American colonists a tangy spruce sap to chew. Later colonists chewed wax.

The gum we chew today had its beginnings in 1869. An unpopular Mexican commander fled from Mexico to Staten Island, New York. He brought with him a chunk of *chicle*, a milky-white gummy substance. He wanted to sell the chicle, which he thought could be made into rubber.

6

Inventors couldn't make rubber out of the chicle. However, one inventor named Thomas Adams discovered that chicle was better to chew than spruce gum or wax. He added the dried root bark of a sassafras tree for taste. Around 1871, he took his invention to a local drugstore, where two gumballs were then sold for a penny. The first modern chewing gum was on the market!

Bubble gum was discovered on August 8, 1928, by Walter Diemar. He had been experimenting for months with different mixes and was surprised when he blew an enormous bubble. The only food coloring he had was pink, so the first bubble gum was pink. Today, bubble gum comes in all colors, but most of it is still pink.

Originally, bubble gum had only one flavor. Today, cinnamon, spearmint, licorice, strawberry, and peppermint are only a few of the many flavors to choose from. What's your favorite flavor?

9

Besides the flavoring, chewing gum has four other basic ingredients: gum base, sugar, corn syrup, and softeners. Gum base won't dissolve, so it holds all the ingredients together. And it's what makes chewing gum chewy. The only difference between bubble gum and chewing gum is in their gum bases—bubble gum's base is firmer and stretchier for good bubble blowing.

10

Gum base was first made from chicle (that same chicle the Mexican commander tried to make into rubber!). Chicle came from the sapodilla tree in Mexico and neighboring countries. When workers made V-shaped cuts in the tree bark, chicle would ooze down the cuts into buckets. The chicle was then boiled, molded into blocks, and sent to the factory.

Natural ingredients are gradually being replaced by synthetic (human-made) ingredients. For example, gum base is now being made with plastics and rubber instead of chicle!

At the factory, all ingredients are stored in large tanks, silos, or bins until it's time to process the gum. Soon they are blended together to create just the right flavor and texture that you love.

Exactly how bubble gum is made is kept a secret, but we *do* know the basic process. First, the gum base is ground up and heated. Then it is dried. Next, it is cooked in large kettles until it is as thick as maple syrup. The cooking sterilizes the gum base.

13

The cooked gum base is put into huge mixing vats, and all the other ingredients are added to it. Sugar sweetens the gum. Corn syrup also sweetens gum and keeps it fresh. Softeners, such as vegetable oils, help blend the ingredients and keep the gum soft and moist.

All these ingredients are mixed together, and the gum is kneaded like bread dough and flattened into sheets. Machines cut the sheets into sticks, gumballs, pellets, or chunks. Finally, the different pieces are covered with powdered sugar to prevent sticking.

15

Once the gum is cut into shapes, other machines wrap the pieces in aluminum foil or paper to keep them fresh and juicy. Then the gum is gathered and sealed in airtight packages. The packages are labeled with the date and the ingredients.

You find all sorts of surprises inside bubble-gum wrappers. Comics, stickers, and baseball cards make great collecting items. And you can make endless gum chains from the wrappers of stick gum. Gumballs, which are not wrapped, are polished with wax, glazed, and branded with edible ink.

During World War II, American soldiers introduced bubble gum to people all over the world. They even gave it to a Stone Age tribe on a Pacific island and to Eskimos in Alaska. The Eskimos enjoyed it so much that they gave up their old tradition of chewing whale blubber. Now bubble gum is found all over the world.

Bubble gum has even been taken up into space. Astronauts on the *Titan 4* smuggled it on board in 1965. Then, a few months later, it was taken officially on the *Titan 5* mission.

There's such a thing as bubble gum manners. Don't chew like a cow, and remember that it isn't polite to blow bubbles everywhere you go. Throw your bubble gum into the trash when you're through with it. If you don't, it may turn up where you don't want it—like the bottom of your shoe or the seat of your pants. Also, it's rude to stick gum on the edge of your plate at mealtime!

There may be times when it isn't too cool to blow bubbles, but remember: you're never too old to learn how.

What do you think happened when that twenty-two-inch bubble, the world's biggest, popped? It probably covered the entire head of the person who blew it! What do you think she did? She probably tried again. Because there's no end to the number of bubbles you can blow with one wad of bubble gum!

ABOUT THE ARTIST

Tom Payne is a freelance illustrator whose illustrations and cartoons appear in national magazines. His work includes travel illustrations for the *National Geographic Traveler*. He lives in upstate New York with his wife, Anne, and his nameless dog.